You Are Old

**Also by
Dr. Oswald T. Pratt and Scott Dikkers**

*You Are Worthless:
Depressing Nuggets of Wisdom
Sure to Ruin Your Day*

You Are
Old

Sobering Affirmations for Your Rapidly Disappearing Life

Dr. Oswald T. Pratt
with Scott Dikkers
and Alexander Blechman

Andrews McMeel Publishing®

Kansas City • Sydney • London

Andrews McMeel Publishing, LLC
an Andrews McMeel Universal company
1130 Walnut Street, Kansas City, Missouri 64106

www.andrewsmcmeel.com

14 15 16 SHO 10 9 8 7 6 5 4

ISBN: 978-1-4494-1839-7

Library of Congress Control Number: 2011944743

Contents

So, You're Going to Die Soon

So, you are old.

You're past your prime. Your best days are behind you. You're over the hill. Your body doesn't bounce back like it used to. It's starting to hurt a lot. You've got a bad back. Your neck has a crink in it. Your knees hurt. You're arthritic. You have rheumatoid arthritis, chronic pain syndrome, bursitis, shingles, hives, cataracts, the bends, and ringworm.

And you've broken your hip.

To the casual observer, you're starting to sag, wrinkle, dry out, hunch over, quiver, dawdle, tire easily, pee in your pants, and forget stuff. You're developing age spots, gray hair, mysterious aches, painful memories, a tremor, a hearing problem, and a slight chill.

You're getting crispy.

No one needs you anymore. Your ideas are out of date. Your opinions antiquated.

Your thoughts overrun with dust and cobwebs. Whenever you open your mouth, children snicker at the silly old fool. Everything you say is a joke now, no matter how earnestly you express yourself. In fact, the more intensely serious you are, the funnier you appear to others. Yours is like a voice from yesteryear that's now only good for a hardy laugh.

You have come to that time in life when you can no longer in good conscience refer to yourself as a "young man" or "young woman."

Soon you will die.

Have you tried to mask your old age? It's not too late. Maybe no one will notice you're old if you dye your hair jet black. Atop your age-spotted head, that will look great. No one will suspect you have the course, stark-white hair of a ghoul, even when it starts coming out in the roots, making you look like some kind of skunk-skeleton.

If you have no hair, consider donning a wig, toupee, hat, or that spray paint they used to advertise on late-night TV infomercials. Try it now while there's still a chance you could fool 1 or even 2 percent of casual observers!

Find out what teenagers are wearing now. I've seen the young men wearing pants that are falling down past their asses. That could be a good look for you that might radiate youth. I've seen teenaged girls dressing like crack whores—maybe you could take up that look as an elderly woman. People will see what you're wearing and never suspect you're not nineteen years old.

I've heard there's some very good plastic surgery you can get that will cover up your wrinkles or stretch out your face until it's like silly putty on a newspaper, with Botox pumped into your lip. Your entire face could be immobilized, with bulbous cheeks infused with poison, swollen as if from the bite of a black widow spider, barely able to move or express any emotion when you speak. Everyone who sees you will marvel at your ageless beauty!

These are some of the tricks used by the rich and famous, and by Hollywood celebrities. And they surely know what works! I recommend you conceal your age through these methods and others—bury yourself deep into denial. You're not old! You're as young as you feel!

Aw, who are we kidding? You're old. Damned old. And there's absolutely no hope for you. The end is near.

Hello. I am licensed therapist Oswald T. Pratt. I'm here to hold your hand along this last leg of your journey through life. I offer the caring embrace of a trained mental health professional. (Please do not track me down where I work to get a real embrace.)

I am a self-help expert who has written a book, so I know what I'm talking about. And I'm here to tell you that everything is going to be alright, once you're gone.

You, on the other hand, will continue to feel more and more decrepit until your last days, and that's normal. Your final experience on this earth will be one of agony—the feeling of every organ in your body failing, your heart giving out, and your last breath wheezed out painfully, well before you have a chance to say anything important. And even if you do eke out some last whimper, no one will hear it. Who wants to listen to the nonsensical ramblings of some old coot?

One thing I can tell you about getting old—no one will be there for you. Except me. Carry this book with you as a handbook—a spirit-guide, if you will. And I will offer sage advice on how to cope with all of the terrible, terrible suffering that awaits you.

Good luck, old person. The road ahead is going to be a nightmare. A feeble, withering, crotchety nightmare of sheer, unadulterated oldness.

And there's nothing you can do about it.

Except get older.

—Oswald T. Pratt, Certified Marriage and Family Therapist

Wrapping Up Your Failed Career

Let the economy be a wondrous scapegoat for your failures in life.

That office humor comic strip you put on your cubicle wall is laughing at you, not with you.

Steal some office supplies before you leave. That'll really stick it to the man.

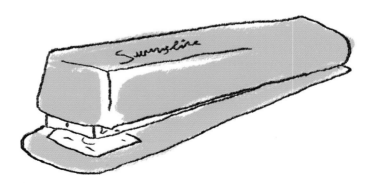

When you die, nobody at your office will attend your funeral. But some of them will read the office-wide e-mail announcing your funeral, and then they will delete it.

Your boss would gladly hunt you for sport.

Don't feel bad about having to wear a nametag. None of the customers even notice it because they don't care who you are.

If it makes you feel better, your smug co-workers will get old and feeble and die of cancer just like you.

YOU ARE OLD

Remember your childhood dreams?
No, I didn't think so.

You would be an astronaut if your parents
had sent you to space camp like you asked.
This is all their fault.

Maybe it's not too late to go to refrigerator repair school.

You would have made more money and dealt with less shit if you had been a plumber.

"Dead-end job" is the wrong analogy for your career. "Car without an engine rolling downhill into a swamp" is more accurate.

Your children will either have worse jobs than you, making you a failure as a parent, or better jobs than you, making you look pathetic by comparison.

Wouldn't it be satisfying to take that stapler and plunge a piece of metal right into the soft fleshy back of your hand? It would hurt a lot, and blood would stream down your arm and drip to the floor, but at least today would be different.

When you run into a co-worker on the street, you've ruined their day by reminding them of work. That's what you are: a sad reminder.

After you retire from your terrible job you will spend all day in your apartment doing nothing. Then one day you will be unable to wipe your ass and your children will put you in a nursing home, where you will continue doing nothing, but in a more depressing environment.

One day you will look back fondly on your awful job as a happy time in your life, because the future is going to be so much worse.

YOU ARE OLD

The stock market, where your retirement funds are, is like a casino doused with kerosene built on top of a volcano.

This is all there is. This is the rest of your life.

You exaggerate your job to your friends. "I'm a regional coordinator." Everyone knows that you're just a drone and you have nothing to do with regions.

Imagine that you have to encounter yourself when you were five years old, and you have to tell your five-year-old self what you'll be when you grow up. Think of a way to describe your job that won't make the child cry.

Your last unemployment check will be more than enough to buy a gun.

YOU ARE OLD

"Get movin'!"

Diet and Exercise Can Make You Feel Months Younger!

By all means go ahead and exercise. But don't delude yourself into thinking exercise will stop the inevitable decay.

Anyone smart would welcome obesity and a fatal heart attack. For fifty years you get to eat all the cheeseburgers and milkshakes you want. Then one day you clutch your chest and keel over dead. It really is the best way to go.

If you exercise for just one hour a day, you will spend 1/24th of your life doing grueling and pointless repetitive tasks. You will never get that time back.

Scientists say broccoli can prevent cancer. In reality cancer laughs at your pitiful broccoli shield. If cancer comes to claim you it'll knock the broccoli aside with one swipe of its mighty tumor-filled tentacle, then devour you whole.

The only diet that works is to not eat anything delicious ever, and spend your entire life feeling hungry and sad.

Everyone at the gym is judging you. And with good reason. You look ridiculous.

The good news is that you'll automatically eat less and get thinner as you grow older, because your metabolism will slow down, and eating more than a few bites will leave you constipated for days.

Pooping will be an accomplishment. Days will go by without a bowel movement.

Your spouse, if still alive, will ask you if your bowel has moved yet. You'll say, "no luck yet, but I'm hopeful for later today."

This is one of the last years you have left to eat what you want without enduring several days of colonic agony.

If you're a woman your boobs will sag. If you're a man you'll get boobs. Then they'll sag.

"Well, you're alive... barely."

Some day medical science will create tiny machines that float in our bloodstream and fix our cells, keeping us young forever. This will happen exactly one year after you die.

"Why did I spend so much time struggling to lift weights" you'll think as you struggle to make it to the bathroom for your weekly poop.

My arms are tired from typing this. I don't know why I even bother.

Go eat some ice cream. It's the only thing that can soothe the pain.

When Are You Old Enough to Be a Racist?

The one silver lining of becoming silver haired is that expectations of you plummet. Societal norms will no longer apply to you if you choose to ignore them.

Feel free to spew all the bigotry you've kept hidden inside for years. You're a decrepit old fool who's going to be dead soon and no one will bother investing the time in telling you how offensive you are.

Everyone knows you're set in your ways now. That's good. Now you never have to change, learn, or grow.

"Now I finally feel entitled to express my deep hatred of all humanity."

It's time to pin all your failures on everyone whose skin is darker than yours.

Filipinos, they've got another thing coming.

Hating everyone who's different will make you feel better about yourself.

The horrors of aging become more bearable if you blame your arthritis on the Mexican nurse who is secretly poisoning you. Be sure to always point out that she is a Mexican.

Now you'll finally be able to tell all those Jewish jokes you pretended to be offended by.

Here's a joke. A rabbi walks into a bar. He hears you saying, "Why did the Jew cross the road? To start all wars." Rather than get angry the rabbi says a prayer for your health, because you look pale and on the verge of death.

I can already hear your indignant harrumphing. "I'm not racist," you tell yourself. "I love all living things and will never take advantage of this gift of bigotry." I'm sorry, but you don't have a choice. You're old now, and all old people are racists.

Can you believe they're giving other people the same rights that you enjoy? It's an outrage!

You may feel proud that you're a relatively tolerant individual, but you're just a product of your times. If you had been born in 1700, you'd be raping a slave right now.

You are a horrible bigot.

"I caught myself saying 'okie doke.'"

You have kept your racism hidden your entire life. Now let it fly, like a beautiful bird.

In the future there will be new kinds of strange and different people for you to be bigoted against. You'll complain, "Cybernetic enhanced humans can't be trusted! Those robo-men only care about serving the cyborg hive mind and assimilating more bionic hatchlings."

And the poor sap charged with pushing your semiconductor-powered wheelchair will say "Sure, you old fart, whatever you say."

"I used the phrase, 'a quarter century ago.'"

When are you old enough to be racist? When you look as though you're pretty much at the end. And in your case that's right now.

Your Children: Will They Give You Money?

"I used the word 'whippersnapper.'"

Your children will never give you money.

All the people who thought their children would take care of them in their golden years are now living in the sewage tunnels under the New York City subway system.

The only reason they call it "the golden years" is because of the loss of bladder control.

Your children can beat you up now.

"I can't even count to how old you are."

You are at their mercy.

Your children feel as though they owe you nothing.

YOU ARE OLD

In fact, they're still asking *you* for money.

Fucking ungrateful little fucks.

If you ever thought your children were a good investment, the laugh's on you.

If you added up all the money you spent on your children in your life, and instead invested it in Google, you would have 4 billion dollars right now. Wouldn't you trade your children for 4 billion dollars? I would.

When the chips are down, your children will take care of themselves, not you.

After they take care of themselves, your children are going to take care of their children. You are not even on the radar.

Why would your children invest in a dying generation?

Aren't you glad your parents are long dead?

"Congratulations! You qualify for our 'Nearly Dead' discount."

Your children are thrilled to take advantage of your barely adequate babysitting skills.

When there's a fire, you'll be the last one to be rescued from the burning house.

Accidental death from smoke inhalation is starting to sound a hell of a lot better than a several-thousand-dollars-a-month nursing home bill.

No one will ever suspect your children purposefully left you to die in the fire.

They've lied to you all their lives. Of course, they're going to lie about your death, too.

They might rescue your pills, though. Those at least have some street value.

Your children hate you.

Here are some things your children call you now:

You-know-who

The insufferable nightmare

Old fart

Old man

Old lady

Grandma

Grandpa

Uncle Jesse

Gramps

Granny

Blue-Hair

**Crumpled-up Shell
of a Former Person**

The Thing That Won't Die

Grandchildren: The Curse That Keeps on Cursing

When your children have children, they will roll their eyes at the mere thought of your coming to visit.

To your grandchildren, all you are is a science experiment to study the effects of aging on facial skin.

Boy, nature sure tricked you good. You thought you were out of the woods with this whole "taking care of children" burden, but there's a whole new generation to clean up after, and your children are happy to drop them off at your doorstep whenever they want a break.

Just what you need: to stoop over and change more diapers.

Grandchildren are the worst thing, ever.

To your grandchildren, you are a mummy.

Make sure your grandchildren know how painful it is for you to dispense all that birthday money.

Fuck the birthday money. Those days are over. You've given out enough money.

And what have you gotten back? A lot of whining, that's what.

The devolution of a pony tail

Tell them, "Now, listen here and listen good—I invested in your mommy or your daddy and gave them birthday money all their lives, and now look at them! They're bone broke and worthless! And they haven't given me anything back. Well, you're going to give me something back, I don't know what, but this money isn't free, you snot-nosed little pest. You owe me! The universe owes me!!"

Nursing Homes Aren't So Bad*

*Yes They Are

Nursing homes get a bad rap in this country. Everyone assumes they're dens of horrible sadness and misery. But they're just buildings. It's the people in them that are horribly sad and miserable.

You have two choices: being decrepit in your house or being decrepit in a nursing home. The only real difference is that if you fall and break your hip in a nursing home an ambulance comes right away, instead of several days later when your kids check to see why you aren't answering the phone.

I can't stress the hip thing enough. Your hip is a ticking time bomb. Sooner or later your hip is going to shatter like a piece of chalk, and a nursing home is the best place for that to happen.

"I always dreamed of one day having my meals in a paper cup."

You are not self-sufficient.

You will never get better.

Admit it. You could use a few burly men to help carry you to the toilet.

You can barely stand.

Your muscles are like dry and brittle string beans.

You need guards to stop you from wandering out the door and into traffic.

You are an imbecile. And I don't mean "dumbass" or "not very bright"; I mean that you cannot perform a simple action like putting your pants on.

Imbeciles need nurses to do their thinking for them. The nice nurse will bring you pills in a cup. Don't ask. Just eat the pills.

If you can't swallow pills on your own the nice nurse will grab your throat, tilt your head back, and force feed you the pills. This is a valuable and helpful service. Those pills will do wonderful things like make you sleep through the last years of your life.

People complain that being in a nursing home is like being in a hospice. They're right. Both are for hopeless dying people who can't do anything on their own.

You can't bathe yourself.

Think how great it will be to get a tray of gruel brought to your room and spoon fed to you.

If you can't afford a nursing home, you'll fall and be trapped on the floor of your living room with a broken hip for days. On day 8, you will eat your own arm to survive.

Count yourself lucky to even be let into a nursing home. I've seen people in nursing homes who look younger than you. You should probably be taken straight to the morgue.

Oh, who am I kidding? Ignore everything I've said in this chapter so far. Nursing homes are abysses of misery.

"Let's go. Time to flush your dignity down the toilet."

Nursing homes are mankind's attempt to defy nature's explicit message that it's time to take your bow and exit stage right.

Are you in a nursing home now? Look out the window. What do you see? Nothing, because you're old, and you can't see.

The Eskimos have it right. It's better to take a brief ride on an ice floe and succumb to peaceful icy sleep than sit for ten years in a rec room watching one channel all day because they don't trust you with the remote.

Someone will be right along to wipe your ass.

The worst part is that they won't necessarily lift you onto the toilet right away. It's like calling your office's IT guy. You have to put in a request to expel your bowels; then if you're lucky someone will swing by in half an hour or so.

When your IT guy is busy, you just have to put up with your broken keyboard for another day and keep pressing the Shift key because Caps Lock isn't working. When your nursing home's orderly is busy, you will befoul your pants and sit in the waste for hours.

Nursing homes are prisons for old people.

Actually, nursing homes are slightly different than prison. There are fewer family visits, no conjugal sex, and the parole board is the Angel of Death.

Just like a real parole board, the Grim Reaper will probably say no several times. The nursing home's round-the-clock care and attention will be just enough to keep you alive and suffering for years.

The kind thing would be to let you die.

This is what you'll say to yourself after failing to die: "Darn it, I thought that stroke was going to be my ticket out of here. But now I'm still alive, and blind also!"

If you try to escape a nursing home, the orderly who gives you enemas will chase after you and tackle you, and you will break your hip.

You can say "Please let me go. I've never seen France and I want to climb the Eiffel Tower before I die" and they will still not let you leave. Why not? Because your children are paying them to hold you captive.

Nursing homes are less like American prisons and more like those prisons that dissidents get sent to in corrupt Middle Eastern countries. It's not that you've committed a crime; it's that your existence is an inconvenience. A dark cell is a great place to put you so that everyone can forget you.

But instead of a dark cell it's brightly lit with buzzing fluorescent lights. The point is the same: Your children hate you and wish you were dead.

You're costing your children money with every second you live. It's not cheap to keep you in your cell.

If execution were an option instead of incarceration, your kids would take it. It'd be doing you a favor, too. The only one coming out ahead here is the nursing home.

Try to do something to die. Even if you don't succeed, it's a fun project that will keep you busy all those years in the nursing home.

There's Still a Chance to Leave Your Mark

Hint: It Involves a Gun and a Lot of People in the Mall

By now you've probably realized that you're not going to accomplish anything.

If you were going to do something great you would have done it a long time ago, in your twenties. That was your best chance.

Most famous people are pretty much established by the time they're twenty-five. How did you do?

Forget winning an Oscar. You'll never even attend the Oscars. You won't even attend the Golden Globes.

YOU ARE OLD

There are no Nobel Prizes in your future. No one in Sweden will ever know your name.

You are not the next Mark Zuckerberg.

Don't even think about becoming an English professor. A whole lot of baristas already have their English PhDs and they're ahead of you in line for the next opening.

You are not the next Warren Buffett. First of all, you're not smart enough to play the markets. Second of all, you're really dumb.

"Any last words?"
"Tell... those damned kids... to get... the hell... off... my lawn."

To recap: You are a failure.

You are a loser.

You have wasted your life.

You're a flash in the pan without the flash or the pan.

Nobody respects you. Nobody disrespects you either, which is worse, because you aren't even crossing their mind. You're just some old person.

You have one last chance to make a name for yourself. And it's killing a whole lot of people.

Now, I'm not telling you to go out and kill a whole lot of people. Encouraging you to do so would be illegal and it could get me in a lot of trouble. This is all just hypothetical. But I challenge you to think of one way of getting your own Wikipedia page that isn't a felony.

You have to choose your style of infamy. Spree, cryptic calling card, or crime of the century. Scratch that last one—too much work.

Spree is a popular choice. It's easy to plan, which is great because you're a lazy mass-murderer.

Just get a gun, go somewhere crowded, and use the gun. That's all there is to it. You've spreed. Congratulations.

A cryptic calling card could be fun. Kill joggers and leave a single rose next to each corpse. You'll be the "Flower Killer" and newspapers will print any letter you mail them. But I doubt you could kill that many joggers without getting caught.

You probably don't have anything interesting to tell newspapers anyway.

Your thimble collection

You definitely can't pull off the crime of the century. That's when you kill someone who's actually successful, like Abraham Lincoln, or steal their baby, like Charles Lindbergh's. I wouldn't even try. The organizational skills needed are beyond you.

Just stick with the spree. I think a spree's more your speed.

Or you could just kill yourself in a public place. You'd probably miss everyone during your spree anyway. Then a cop would shoot you in the thigh and you'd go to prison and be a pathetic, old, crippled prisoner.

Killing yourself in public would probably get you a mention on the local news. Not too shabby.

I wouldn't shoot yourself though. You'd probably shoot yourself in a nonlethal part of the brain and end up a drooling vegetable.

Jump from way up high. Gravity can get the job done even if you can't.

Good luck. I'll keep my TV on Fox-5 and hope to see you.

YOU ARE OLD

Your Body: Now More Disgusting Than Ever

Your physical body is a revolting, shriveled-up husk that you should shield from public view.

No one wants to look at any part of you. Use pastel button-down sweaters, long slacks, and summer hats as tarps to drape over your unsightly body.

Gray hairs are your mold.

So is ear hair.

Your brittle, age-spotted skin means you are now more lizard than human.

And your genitals are hideous.

Are you fat also? Good for you. Perhaps your fat belly conceals your genitals.

You have flappy jowls.

"Do you still think I'm pretty?"

"No, I do not."

They could make a horror movie out of your body:

Wrinkles, Wrinkles Everywhere!

Attack of the Age-Spot Blob

Dawn of the Almost Dead

On Golden Pond

The Bucket List 2: You Didn't Do Any of the Things On Your List and Now You're Dead

Dating After 40: Good Luck with That

When you're on a date, remember that people don't like to see public displays of affection, especially from two disgusting old people in love.

You may think you're in love, but you're really just desperately clinging to another life in your final moment before death.

Be careful sharing a malted milk with your date. You may catch Alzheimer's.

Perhaps you could go to the nursing home den to watch *Jeopardy!* on your next date.

Many of the people in your little black book are now dead.

Ah, Sex. Maybe you can stir up a vague memory of what it was like.

There's a thing you used to do with another person in intimate moments. Fight through the fog and haze of your senility and try to picture it.

Wait—be sure to picture yourself young, not old!

Too late. You imagined yourself old having sex.

YOU ARE OLD

You are disgusting.

Be ashamed.

Run and hide in a cave on the outskirts of town.

We can only hope the torch-wielding towns-people will storm your cave and demand that you come out so they can burn you to death.

It will be really sexy when your incontinence is introduced in the bedroom.

Oh,
the Places
You Won't
Go!

Here's a list of all the things you used to be able to do but will likely never do again, because you're old:

play

run

jump

hop

skip

jump rope

skinny dip

streak

swim

hip-hop

sock hop

jitterbug

breakdance

a pull-up

a push-up

a chin-up

win the Iron Cross

the Ironman Triathlon

a world record for fitness

skin your knee

look good in the mirror

march

hyperventilate

have hot sex

feel "younger than ever"

feel great

take in a deep breath and say
"Ah, it's good to be young"

hurdle

hula hoop

Things You'll Never, Ever Do Again

(continued)

play round robin

play musical chairs

race

play Operation

play Candyland

play Sorry

play Clue

jump in a pile of leaves

jump into the ol' swimmin' hole

swing on a tire swing

laugh

enjoy your life

find something exciting on the beach

get excited by the date on a penny

fall in love

do a jig

sing a limerick

be a maverick

tell a joke

laugh

feel the wind in your hair

play chicken

be lost on a desert island with a model

get spanked

run through a sprinkler

run through the rain

run on the beach

run

ride a tandem bicycle

fly a kite

walk barefoot in the grass

sing

exclaim, "Oh it's great to be alive"

get an Indian burn

play "2 minutes in the closet"

get locked in the closet

get beaten up

get a new toy

play with a toy

get a birthday card

remember to send a birthday card

blow up a balloon

run around

get into trouble

piss off Old Man Jameson

get yelled at to get off the lawn

try the latest recreational drug

learn the new dance step

use a computer

get a Twitter account

go to the bathroom by yourself

be happy

"I used to know how to do that..."

So You're Rich Enough to Retire. You Bastard.

You are a responsible investor who has made very wise choices, and you make me want to vomit.

I hate you.

Live it up, Thurston, because you're probably going to get cancer and die the day after you officially retire. At least, I hope you do.

You saved all your pennies and invested them wisely. That was a nerdy thing to do. You are a pathetic nerd who is good at math.

"We're sorry to inform you that your retirement account has been accidentally deleted."

You're set up with a comfortable annuity or pension or some other financial thing that I don't understand. I suppose you think that makes you smarter than me.

You are not smarter than me. You may be smart in this one area, but in every other area you are *stupid!*

Why didn't you tell me about these grow-in-to-a-rich-person money trees? Why do you hate me?

Did you set all that retirement stuff up for me, too? *Why not?!*

You effectively *stole* from me by not telling me about all this stuff and not forcing me to do it.

I will have you arrested. Is that citizen's arrest thing for real? Can a citizen really just arrest anybody else? God, I am thrilled but also terrified by that.

Could you at least explain to me how to properly save for retirement? It's all very confusing and I never really followed it.

Could you also please invent a time machine so that I can go back in time and start investing $200 a month while in my twenties so I can be smart like you?

Maybe you could just set me up with one of those mutual accounts or some other kind of huge pile of money I could have?

Just give me a bunch of your money and we'll call it fair.

Can I please have your money?

Give me your money.

"We regret to inform you that as soon as you turn 59 and a half, the new 'Retirement Savings Don't Count' Law will go into effect."

Maybe just cut back on your golf game or chamber orchestra tickets and old-person skin treatments and send me like $50 every month.

That's less than $2 a day.

Your gift will help feed someone who is hungry. And sad. And lonely. And poor. And old.

I'm tired of trying to cajole you using reason. Just give me some of your damned money!

You selfish prick.

Waaaah! I want what you have!! I want money!! Waaah!

Hey, at least I *enjoyed* spending all my money. Wait, I guess I've been pretty miserable most of my life. You *bastard!*

Your DVD Collection and More: The Few Things You're Proud Of

Life is short, bleak, and ends the same way it began: with a puddle of bodily fluids leaking from someone's groin.

Children are told they can do anything they want. Accomplish farfetched dreams like becoming the first female astronaut president ballerina who pitches for the New York Yankees while ending world hunger. But in the eye blink of life there is no time for most people to become "successful" or "happy." All we can realistically hope for is to avoid becoming a complete loser.

Rather than judge yourself by some ridiculous standard of wealth, fame, or professional success, instead rate yourself by how you could have fucked up a *lot* worse.

You're definitely not a winner in the game of life, but maybe you're not a complete loser either. Maybe you're merely a partial loser.

Look back on your life. You'll see that you've actually done some things you can be proud of. Well, let's be honest. They were small victories, at best. Actually, they are weak and pathetic excuses for a life.

Such as . . .

Your DVD collection is large and impressive. After your death your surviving kin might actually argue about who gets to keep it. Unfortunately, you will die just as DVDs become obsolete.

Your semidecent Christopher Walken impression makes you entertaining for a glorious eight seconds at every party.

You visited the Leaning Tower of Pisa without pretending to hold it up.

You resisted masturbating to a photo of a kidnapped college kid shown on the news.

By the age of ten, without any help, you discovered that Coke and Sprite can be combined into the delicious lemon-lime cola Sproke.

When your pet hermit crab outgrows its shell you always have a larger replacement shell waiting and ready for him.

You solved one whole face of a Rubik's cube.

After reading *Catcher in the Rye,* you resisted incorporating "phony" into your vocabulary of commonly used words. People like that should be shot.

You don't use the phrase "people like that should be shot." People who say that should be shot. Yes, I should be shot.

You should also be shot.

At least one time in your life you've had sexual intercourse with someone who didn't demand money. Yes, a prostitute giving her regular customer a birthday freebie counts.

You were born with eyeballs.

You are reasonably confident that if you tied a noose it could support the weight of a human being of your size without coming undone.

Your home is just normal disgusting, not *Hoarders* disgusting.

You realize that bars are for suckers and save money by drinking alone at home.

You have had some very healthy bowel movements.

Your hair is thinning, but at least your hideous, bare scalp is free of boils.

Your wallet contains more than $2 right now. Although you are poor, you're at least "can-buy-a-soda poor."

You do not work in a hog-fat rendering plant.

Charismatic and attractive people don't laugh at you behind your back. In fact, they are completely unaware of your existence.

While you have gotten drunk and blacked out many times, you have never drowned in your own vomit.

Local teens don't play pranks on your house. That's because they think you're a serial killer, but for once this is to your advantage.

You may have no friends, but at least your television loves you.

When you die, a decent handful of people will feel obligated to attend your funeral.

At least one of your friends is a more pathetic loser than you.

Your excellent taste in hats partially counteracts your hideous, bloated appearance.

Although frail and hideous, your body is not yet filled with incurable tumors.

You've successfully kept your true self hidden from your friends and family.

You Have Nothing to Look Forward To

Your life is pretty much over.

There's nothing exciting on your horizon but pain, forgetfulness, and general decline.

Oh, but did you hear about that great new movie that's coming out next summer? Wait, never mind. You'll be dead.

Bet you can't wait to get to the surprise twist ending in that new book you're reading. Too bad you'll die before you get there.

So-and-so is going to have a baby? How wonderful! Maybe you can send a gift from the grave.

Since you are too old and crippled to get out of your Craftmatic adjustable bed and fill up a watering jug, you can look forward to watching all of your plants die.

Maybe you'll see one of your good friends again before you die. But probably not.

All of your friends are dead.

Who's going to feed your cat after you die?! Aw, who cares?

Of course, you have Heaven to look forward to. You're going to get a robe and walk around on golden walkways and learn to play the harp for all of eternity. This is really going to happen!

You can look forward to getting sick and fucking tired of listening to harp music.

You can look forward to boll weevils and maggots devouring your flesh for all of eternity.

At least you won't have to listen to the chuckles and snickers when they read your will.

You have no future.

Your fate is in the hands of the healthcare system.

Not Much Time Left . . .

It's time to welcome the sweet release of death.

If this were the year 1270, you would be dead already.

Why are you still alive?

Tick... tick... tick... tick....

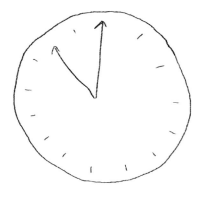

You have overstayed your welcome.

Haven't you had just about enough of this "life" crap?

I think I can speak for everyone when I say we are sick and tired of seeing you breathe.

Time's up. Time to be dead now.

You have lived too long.

Let today be the first day of the end of your life.

Aaaalmost dead . . .

Keep looking at your watch. Why are you still alive?

Did you draw another breath just now? Surely this next one will be your last.

Please lie down so that you don't hurt anyone or knock over something valuable when you drop dead.

Please give me some of your money before you die. I could really use it!

Your arthritic old hands can barely hold on to this book.

The book has fallen to the nursing room floor. You aren't reading this anymore.

You are slumped over, a line of drool dangling from your lower lip.

Good-bye! You are finally dead.

Epilogue

**You are now
a mess that
someone has
to clean up.**